Birds Need Trees – Trees Need Birds

Written by Margaret MacDonald

Picture Dictionary

food

insects

nest

seeds

shelter

tree

Look at this tree.
You can see the trunk.
You can see branches.
Can you see the birds
in the tree, too?

leaves

flowers

This bird is making a home
on a branch.
It is building a nest.
Most birds
need trees to nest in.

twigs

grass

This bird is in a tree.
It is sheltering from the sun.
Birds shelter
from wind and rain
in trees, too.
Birds need trees for shelter.

Birds need trees for food.
Birds find many things
to eat in trees.
Some birds eat nectar.
Some birds eat insects.

grub

blossom

Trees need birds, too.
When birds eat fruit,
they carry some seeds
from the tree
to another place.
They drop the seeds
and new trees grow.

fig

flesh

Some insects harm trees.
They eat the leaves.
Birds eat insects
that can harm trees.

caterpillar

hole

Activity Page

Make a list of the things that birds need trees for.

Do you know the dictionary words?